I0012178

"PYTHON BRILLIANCE: A GENIUS'S GUIDE TO MASTERY AND BEYOND"

Contents

8

Presentation

Welcome to "Python for Virtuoso Personalities" - a complete aide created for the people who look for dominance in the craft of Python programming. You've come to the right place if you're an enthusiast, an experienced developer, or just a curious mind who likes to push the boundaries of Python's capabilities.

1. Outline of Python's Splendor

Python is something beyond a programming language; It serves as a platform for creative thinking and problem-solving. Its straightforwardness and clarity make it open to fledglings, however its extensibility and adaptability draw in the most splendid personalities in the field. In this aide, we will dive into the profundities of Python, investigating progressed ideas, state of the art strategies, and best practices that go past the common.

2. Why Python for Virtuoso Personalities?

Python has turned into the most widely used language of the programming scene, and for good explanation. Its exquisite language structure and huge environment engage engineers to handle a large number of difficulties, from web improvement to AI and then some. In this aide, we plan to raise your Python ability, giving you the devices and information to compose code that functions as well as features genuine virtuoso.

3. What to expect this guide is not for the timid.

We will explore through the mind boggling domains of Python, unwinding its insider facts and uncovering the power it holds for those ready to investigate. Each part is made to give both hypothetical comprehension and active experience, guaranteeing that you embrace the ideas as well as can apply them in certifiable situations.

Whether you're hoping to improve your abilities, develop your comprehension, or just extinguish your hunger for information, "Python for Virtuoso Personalities" is your buddy on this excursion to Python dominance.

Prepare yourself for an exciting journey through the realms of Python that will test your mind, expand your horizons, and ultimately make you a Python virtuoso.

Allow the excursion to start!

Groundworks of Python Authority

In the tremendous scene of Python, fabricating a strong groundwork is fundamental for accomplishing genuine dominance. You will learn about advanced data types, functional programming concepts, and the fundamental building blocks of Python expertise in this section.

1. High level Information Types

1.1 Sets, Tuples, and Namedtuples

Investigate the complexities of sets, tuples, and namedtuples. Comprehend their utilization cases, unchanging nature, and how to use them for effective information control.

1.2 High level Records and Rundown Understandings

Plunge profound into records and saddle their power with cutting edge strategies, including list understandings, cutting, and controlling settled records.

2. Concepts of Functional Programming

2.1: Lambda Functions With lambda expressions, discover the elegance of anonymous functions. Figure out how to utilize them actually for succinct and expressive code.

2.2 Higher-Request Capabilities
Excel at higher-request capabilities, understanding how capabilities can be passed as contentions and returned as values.

2.3 Decorators and Terminations
Dive into decorators and terminations, two strong elements

that improve code seclusion and viability. Figure out how to apply these ideas in true situations.

3. Classes and Objects in Object-Oriented Python

3.1 Explore the concepts of encapsulation, inheritance, and polymorphism for a comprehensive comprehension of classes and objects.

3.2 Legacy and Polymorphism
Figure out how to make adaptable and versatile code by dominating legacy and polymorphism.

3.3 Metaclasses and Class Decorators
Release the maximum capacity of Python's article arranged abilities by investigating metaclasses and class decorators. Learn how these

advanced features can influence your classes' behavior.

Building areas of strength for an is the most vital move towards Python dominance. You will not only improve your comprehension of Python as you progress through these advanced concepts, but you will also lay the groundwork for tackling more complex problems in subsequent sections. Prepare to raise your Python abilities higher than ever!

Dominating Item Arranged Python

In the domain of Python programming, dominating item arranged ideas is vital for making strong, adaptable, and viable code. This part will direct you through the complexities of classes, legacy, polymorphism, and high level item situated methods.

1. Classes and Items

1.1 Grasping Classes

Class Definition: Gain proficiency with the essentials of characterizing classes and making objects.

Properties and Strategies: Investigate how to characterize qualities and techniques inside a class.

1.2 Example Factors and Strategies

Example Factors: Learn more about the role that instance variables play in object-oriented design.

Methods: Grasp various kinds of strategies, including occasion techniques, class techniques, and static strategies.

2. Legacy and Polymorphism

2.1 Legacy in Python

Base Classes and Inferred Classes: Create base and derived classes to learn about inheritance.

Strategy Abrogating: Learn how to customize derived classes by overriding their methods.

2.2 Polymorphism

Polymorphic Way of behaving: Comprehend how polymorphism permits objects of various sorts to be treated as objects of a typical kind.

Duck writing: Investigate Python's dynamic composing and how it adds to polymorphic way of behaving.

3. Composition and Aggregation:

Advanced Object-Oriented Techniques

3.1 Composition: Excel at making complex items by joining easier ones.

Aggregation: Figure out how to make connections between objects utilizing conglomeration.

3.2 Class Decorators and Metaclasses Metaclasses: Investigate metaclasses and their job in altering class creation.

Class Decorators: Comprehend how class decorators can be utilized to change or expand the way of behaving of classes.

4. Configuration Examples in Python

4.1 Creational Examples

Singleton Example: Execute the singleton example to guarantee a class has just a single occurrence.

Processing plant Technique: Learn how to create objects by utilizing the factory method pattern.

4.2 Underlying Examples

Decorator Example: Execute the decorator example to broaden the way of behaving of articles progressively.

Composite Example: Investigate the composite example for taking care of tree designs of articles.

4.3 Personal conduct standards

Onlooker Example: Carry out the spectator example to characterize a one-to-numerous reliance between objects.

System Example: Learn how the strategy pattern defines and makes interchangeable a family of algorithms.

Dominating item arranged Python isn't just about grasping punctuation; about taking on a mentality works with measured and extensible code. As you progress through this segment, you'll acquire the abilities expected to plan and carry out refined arrangements utilizing Python's strong article situated worldview. We should dive into the craft of making rich and powerful article situated Python code!

Advanced Python Techniques In this section, we'll look at advanced Python features and techniques that go beyond the basics to help you write code that is more powerful, expressive, and efficient. From setting chiefs to offbeat programming, this segment will furnish you with the abilities to handle complex situations and advance your Python programs.

1. Setting Supervisors

1.1 The with Articulation

Prologue to Setting Supervisors: Learn about context managers and how they work in resource management and cleanup.

Making Custom Setting Chiefs: Utilizing the contextlib module, learn how to develop your very own context managers.

2. Generators and Iterators

2.1 Generator Capabilities

Figuring out Generators: Investigate the idea of generators and how they contrast from customary capabilities.

Lethargic Assessment: Figure out how generators empower languid assessment and further develop memory effectiveness.

2.2 Coroutines and Asyncio

Prologue to Coroutines: Comprehend offbeat programming

and how coroutines contrast from normal capabilities.

Framework for Asyncio: Plunge into the asyncio module for nonconcurrent I/O tasks and occasion driven programming.

3. Numerous Dispatch with Functools

3.1 Single versus Numerous Dispatch

Grasping Dispatch: Investigate the idea of dispatch and what it means for capability conduct.

Polymorphism with Functools: Learn how to use the functools module to achieve multiple dispatch.

4. Dynamic Composing and Duck Composing

Dynamic Composing in Python: Learn how Python's dynamic typing lets you code with more freedom.

Duck Composing Standards: Write code that takes into account an object's behavior rather than its type, adhering to the "duck typing" philosophy.

5. Execution Advancement Methods

5.1 Profiling and Timing

Profiling Your Code: Learn how to identify performance bottlenecks by utilizing profiling tools.

Timing and Benchmarking: Investigate methods for estimating the execution season of various pieces of your code.

5.2 Cython and Without a moment to spare Gathering

Prologue to Cython: Comprehend how Cython can be utilized to work on the exhibition of Python code.

Pythonic Code Practices

Pythonic code isn't just about composing utilitarian projects; about sticking to the sayings and standards make Python code exquisite, comprehensible, and proficient. This part will direct you through the prescribed procedures and shows that describe Pythonic code, guaranteeing your projects are right as well as a delight to peruse and keep up with.

1. PEP 8 Style Guide

1.1 Space and Organizing

Steady Space: Figure out the significance of reliable space for further developed code lucidness.

Line Length and Wrapping: Stick to Enthusiasm 8 proposals on line length and code wrapping.

1.2 Variable and function naming conventions: Follow Python's naming shows to make your code more coherent and simple.

Class Naming: Figure out the shows for naming classes and keep away from normal entanglements.

2. Composing Colloquial Python Code

2.1 Rundown Perceptions

Making Succinct Records: Become amazing at list appreciations for succinct and expressive code.

Restrictive Rundown Understandings: Utilize restrictive articulations inside list perceptions for more mind boggling sifting.

2.2 Word references and Sets

Word reference Maxims: Investigate colloquial ways of controlling word references for effective information handling.

Operations on a Set: Influence set activities for normal assignments like tracking down exceptional components and set contrasts.

3. Utilizing Pythonic Examples

3.1 EAFP versus LBYL

Simpler to Request Pardoning than Authorization (EAFP): Comprehend and apply the EAFP guideline for cleaner and more powerful code.

LBYL, or look before you leap: Know when to use EAFP and when to use LBYL in situations where it might be appropriate.

3.2 Pythonic Emphasis

Utilizing identify: Learn how to iterate over sequences with index and value by using enumerate.

zip Capability: Investigate the force of the zip capability for emphasizing over various successions in equal.

4. Exception Handling in Pythonic Error Handling

4.1 Proper Use of Exceptions: Comprehend when and how to involve exemptions for dealing with blunders smoothly.

Custom Special cases: Make custom exemptions for explicit blunder cases in your applications.

5. Guarded Programming

5.1 Information Approval

Approving Client Information: Execute vigorous information approval procedures to guarantee your program handles client input nimbly.

Checking the Type: Influence type clues and type actually taking a look at instruments for better code unwavering quality.

By embracing Pythonic code rehearses, you not just make your code more coherent and viable yet in addition adjust your coding style with the more extensive Python people group. As you investigate these practices, you'll acquire a more profound appreciation for the excellence and straightforwardness that characterizes Pythonic code. We should set out on an excursion to compose Python code that fills in as well as does as such in the most potential Pythonic way!

Useful Programming in Python

Utilitarian writing computer programs is a worldview that stresses the utilization of unadulterated capabilities, changelessness, and revelatory articulations. While Python isn't absolutely practical, it integrates useful programming ideas that can improve code lucidity and viability. This segment will direct you through the standards of useful programming in Python and how to successfully use them.

1. Top notch Capabilities

1.1 Regarding Capabilities as Top notch Residents

Doling out Capabilities to Factors: Comprehend how capabilities can be allocated to factors, considering adaptability in code structure.

Passing Capabilities as Contentions: Investigate the force of passing capabilities as contentions to different capabilities.

1.2 Returning Functions from Functions Functions: Figure out how capabilities can return different capabilities, empowering the formation of higher-request capabilities.

2. Permanent Information Designs

2.1 Working with Permanent Sorts

Permanent Implicit Sorts: Investigate unchanging sorts, for example, tuples and strings and grasp their part in practical programming.

Making Unchanging Classes: Figure out how to make custom classes with changeless properties.

3. Recursion and Memorization

3.1 Recursive Capabilities

Grasping Recursion: Ace the idea of recursion and when to involve it for tackling issues.

Optimization of Tail Recursion: Investigate methods for enhancing tail-recursive functions.

3.2 Memoization

Storing with Memoization: Carry out memoization procedures to upgrade recursive capabilities and decrease excess calculations.

Utilizing functools.lru_cache: A built-in memoization solution can be obtained by utilizing the functools module.

4. Higher-Request Capabilities

4.1 Guide, Channel, and Diminish

Map: Apply a capability to all components of an iterable utilizing the guide capability.

Filter: With the filter function, you can filter elements based on a particular condition.

Reduce: Consolidate components of an iterable into a solitary worth utilizing the functools.reduce capability.

4.2 Generator Expressions and List Comprehensions List Comprehensions: Create code for making lists that is both clear and concise.

Generator Articulations: Influence generator articulations for sluggish assessment and memory proficiency.

5. Useful Programming Libraries

5.1 functools Module

Incomplete Capabilities: The functools.partial function is used to create partial functions.

Practical Decorators: Comprehend how to utilize practical decorators for changing the way of behaving of capabilities.

5.2 itertools Module.

Information Science and AI with Python

In the time of information driven navigation, Python has turned into a force to be reckoned with for information science and AI. You will learn how to use essential Python libraries and techniques in this section to analyze data, create predictive models, and gain useful insights.

1. Pandas and NumPy for Data Manipulation

1.1 The Fundamentals of NumPy Arrays and Operations: Learn about broadcasting, vectorized operations, and NumPy arrays.

Direct Polynomial math with NumPy: Investigate straight variable based math activities given by NumPy.

1.2 Pandas DataFrames

DataFrames and Series: Understand how to use Pandas DataFrames and Series.

Information Cleaning and Preprocessing: Handle missing information, copies, and perform information preprocessing assignments.

2. High level Information Representation with Matplotlib and Seaborn

2.1 Matplotlib Basics

Essential Plots: Make line plots, dissipate plots, and bar plots with Matplotlib.

Altering Plots: Put labels, titles, and colors on plots to make them look how you want them to.

Statistical Plots: Seaborn for Statistical Visualization Use Seaborn to make educational measurable representations.

Match Plots and Heatmaps: Imagine connections between factors utilizing pair plots and heatmaps.

3. Supervised Learning Classification:

An Overview of Scikit-learn 3.1 Machine Learning Assemble and assess characterization models for anticipating clear cut results.

Regression: Execute relapse models for anticipating ceaseless factors.

3.2 Clustering of Unsupervised Learning: Investigate grouping calculations to distinguish designs in unlabeled information.

Reduction of Dimensions: Use strategies like PCA for lessening the dimensionality of information.

Cross-Validation of Model Evaluation and Hyperparameter Tuning: Recognize the significance of cross-validation in the evaluation of a robust model.

Lattice Search and Irregular Pursuit: Tuning hyperparameters can improve the performance of the model.

4. Time Series Investigation with Python

4.1 Time Series Rudiments

Time Series Information Dealing with: Handle time series information utilizing Pandas.

Resampling and Collection: Resample time series information and perform conglomeration.

4.2 Time Series Anticipating

ARIMA Models: Investigate AutoRegressive Coordinated Moving Normal (ARIMA) models for time series estimating.

Occasional Deterioration: Separate trend, seasonal, and residual components from time series data.

39

5. Profound Learning with TensorFlow and Keras

5.1 Prologue to Brain Organizations

Building Brain Organizations: Utilize TensorFlow and Keras to fabricate basic brain organizations.

Actuation Capabilities and Analyzers: Comprehend enactment capabilities and streamlining agents in brain organizations.

5.2 Convolutional Brain Organizations (CNNs)

Picture Grouping with CNNs: For image classification tasks, use CNNs.

Transfer of Knowledge: For transfer learning, make use of pre-trained models.

6. Regular Language Handling (NLP) with NLTK and spaCy

6.1 Text Handling and Examination

Tokenization and Stemming: Preprocess text information

utilizing tokenization and stemming.

Text Vectorization: Convert text information into mathematical vectors for AI.

6.2 Named Substance Acknowledgment (NER)

NER with spaCy: Perform Named Substance Acknowledgment utilizing the spaCy library.

Text Characterization with NLP: Assemble text characterization models utilizing NLP strategies.

7. Certifiable Applications and Contextual analyses

7.1 Prescient Investigation

Client Agitate Forecast: Create a model that can predict customer churn in a business environment.

Monetary Estimating: Use time series investigation for monetary guaging.

7.2 Picture Acknowledgment

Object Discovery: Execute models for object location in pictures.

Facial Acknowledgment: Assemble facial acknowledgment frameworks utilizing profound learning.

7.3 Normal Language Handling Applications

Opinion Examination: Utilize NLP methods to examine sentiment in text data.

Chatbot Advancement: Utilize natural language processing to create a straightforward chatbot.

Information science and AI are huge and dynamic fields, and this part means to furnish you with a strong groundwork to investigate and apply these ideas utilizing Python. As you progress through these subjects, you'll acquire the abilities expected to handle certifiable information difficulties and fabricate insightful frameworks. We should leave on an excursion into the intriguing universe of information science and AI with Python!

Synchronization and Parallelism in Python

Actually managing synchronous and equivalent tasks is critical for enhancing execution in current applications. There are a few ways to deal with simultaneousness and parallelism in Python, allowing you to write code that runs faster from there. In this portion, we will examine hanging, multiprocessing, and nonconcurrent programming in Python.

1. Hanging and Multiprocessing

1.1 Hanging in Python

Introduction to Strings: Sort out the fundamentals of strings and their usage in Python.

String Synchronization: Research procedures for synchronizing strings to avoid race conditions.

Overall Go between Lock (GIL): In Python, learn about GIL and how it affects string-based simultaneousness.

1.2 Multiprocessing in Python

Preamble to Multiprocessing: Investigate the multiprocessing module to run various cycles immediately.

Shared Memory and Between process Correspondence (IPC): Appreciate how cycles pass on and share data.

2. Unconventional Programming with Asyncio

2.1 Nonconcurrent I/O

Preface to Asyncio: The Asyncio library will help you become familiar with the fundamentals of nonconcurrent programming.

Coroutines and Event Circles: Research coroutines and event circles for unconventional task execution.

2.2 Language structure of Async/Anticipate Async/Anticipate Examples: Use the async/expect etymological design for creating unique code.

Similarity with Asyncio: Learn how to use Asyncio to complete asynchronous tasks simultaneously.

3. GIL and Improvement of Execution

3.1 Global Translator Lock (GIL) Understanding GIL: Plunge further into the Overall Go between Lock and its impact on multi-hung programs.

Eliminating Obstacles to the GIL: Look into ways to get around GIL restrictions in CPU- and I/O-bound tasks.

3.2 Procedures for Execution Streamlining Profiling and Enhancement: Use profiling gadgets to perceive execution bottlenecks.

Cython and at the last possible second Collection: Upgrade essential areas of code using Cython and JIT gathering.

4. Concurrence Models and Best Practices

4.1 String Prosperity and Locking

Ensuring String Prosperity: Do string safe code using locks and other synchronization parts.

Pause and Race Condition Revultion: Fathom and moderate ordinary synchronization issues.

4.2 Concurrent Destinies

ThreadPoolExecutor and ProcessPoolExecutor: The concurrent.futures module can be used to equalize the execution of errands.

Dealing with Extraordinary cases in Synchronous Tasks: Sort out some way to manage exclusions in synchronous programming.

5. Nonconcurrent Web Frameworks

5.1 Construction Nonconcurrent Web Applications

Preface to Nonconcurrent Web Frameworks: For the advancement of nonconcurrent web applications, explore structures like Quart and FastAPI.

Managing Unconventional Sales: Execute odd sales managing for additional created web application execution.

Synchronization and parallelism are key thoughts for building versatile and responsive applications. By overwhelming these strategies in Python, you'll be ready to plan and complete world class execution structures that can gainfully manage a huge number of concurrent endeavors. We ought to hop into the universe of concurrent and equivalent programming in Python!

Web Advancement with Carafe and Django in Python

Web improvement is a strong use case for Python, and two well known systems, Cup and Django, offer various ways to deal with building web applications. This segment will direct you through the essentials of both Flagon and Django, permitting you to make dynamic and vigorous web applications.

1. Flagon Web Advancement

1.1 Prologue to Flagon

Setting Up a Flagon Task: Make an essential Carafe project structure.

Directing and Perspectives: Characterize courses and perspectives for dealing with HTTP demands.

Layouts and Jinja2: Use Jinja2 templating motor for dynamic substance delivering.

1.2 Taking care of Structures and Client Information

Structure Dealing with in Carafe: Process client input involving Flagon WTF for structure approval.

Security from CSRF: Execute Cross-Site Solicitation Phony assurance in Cup.

1.3 Carafe and Information bases

Joining with SQLite or SQLAlchemy: Connect databases to Flask applications.

Model-View-Regulator (MVC) Engineering: Comprehend and execute MVC in Carafe.

1.4 Flask Extensions An Overview of Flask Extensions: For more features like authentication and RESTful APIs, look into popular Flask extensions.

Getting Flagon Applications: Execute safety efforts, including secret key hashing and validation.

2. Django Web Improvement

2.1 Django Essentials

Making a Django Task: Set up a Django project and comprehend the venture structure.

Django Models and ORM: Define models and make use of the Django ORM to interact with databases.

2.2 Django Perspectives and Formats

Django Perspectives: Execute perspectives to deal with HTTP demands.

Django Formats: For rendering dynamic content, make use of the Django template language.

2.3 User Authentication and Django Forms

Django Forms: Process client input utilizing Django structures for approval.

Client Validation: Execute client verification and approval.

2.4 Django Administrator Board

Django Administrator Connection point: For simple content management, look into the Django admin panel that is already included.

Modifying Administrator Board: Redo and expand the Django administrator board for explicit application needs.

3. Building Relaxing APIs

3.1 Flagon Soothing APIs

Making Relaxing Endpoints in Cup: Execute Soothing APIs utilizing Carafe Peaceful.

Validation and Approval: With authorization and authentication, protect API endpoints.

3.2 Django REST Structure

Prologue to Django REST Structure (DRF): Use DRF to assemble strong and adaptable APIs.

Serializers and Perspectives: Carry out serializers and perspectives for dealing with Programming interface demands.

4. Testing and Sending

4.1 Testing in Jar and Django

Unit Testing: Compose and run unit tests for Cup and Django applications.

Combination Testing: Carry out coordination tests to guarantee the legitimate working of the whole application.

4.2 Options for Deployment Flask Application Deployment: Examine the various Flask application deployment options.

Conveying Django Applications: Convey Django applications

utilizing stages like Heroku, AWS, or Docker.

5. Certifiable Applications and Best Practices

5.1 Prescribed procedures in Web Advancement

Code Construction and Association: Follow best practices for arranging code in enormous web applications.

Documentation and Remarks: Archive your code and follow best practices for composing viable code.

5.2 Genuine Models

Building a Contributing to a blog Stage: Execute key highlights of a publishing content to a blog stage utilizing Cup or Django.

Internet business Application: Create an e-commerce application with features like a shopping cart, user authentication, and product listings.

Web improvement with Cup and Django makes the way for building many applications, from basic sites to complex web frameworks. By dominating these systems, you'll be prepared to plan and carry out unique, versatile, and secure web applications utilizing Python. How about we leave on the excursion of web advancement with Cup and Django!

High level Subjects in Python

This segment covers a scope of cutting edge subjects in Python, investigating ideas that go past the essentials and dig into the complexities of the language. From metaprogramming to composing Python C augmentations, these points will develop your comprehension and empower you to handle complex difficulties.

1. Metaprogramming and Code Reflection

1.1 Decorators and Metaclasses

Making Decorators: Comprehend and make decorators for adjusting or expanding the way of behaving of capabilities.

Metaclasses: Plunge into metaclasses, investigating their part in altering class creation and conduct.

1.2 Code Reflection: Runningtime Code Inspection: Utilize the review module to inspect and control code objects.

Dynamic Code Age: Produce and execute code powerfully founded on runtime conditions.

2. Understanding the Import System:

Customizing Python's Import System Investigate how Python's import framework functions.

Custom Import Snares: Make custom import snares to alter the default import conduct.

3. Writing C Extensions for Python

An Overview of C Extensions: Comprehend the requirement for and advantages of composing C expansions in Python.

Involving Cython for C Augmentations: Influence Cython to improve on the method involved with composing C augmentations.

Execution Streamlining with C Augmentations: Execute execution basic capabilities in C for further developed speed.

4. Testing and Test-Driven Improvement (TDD)

Prologue to Test-Driven Improvement: Embrace TDD standards for composing solid and viable code.

Unit Testing in Python: Utilize the unittest or pytest structure for composing and running tests.

Ridiculing and Test Pairs: Execute taunts and test copies for disengaging code during testing.

5. Documentation Procedures

Composing Successful Documentation: Gain proficiency with the craft of composing clear and compact documentation for your tasks.

Sphinx Documentation Instrument: Use Sphinx to produce proficient looking documentation for your Python projects.

6. Code Audit Methods

Powerful Code Surveys: Comprehend the significance of code surveys in a cooperative improvement climate.

Code Linting and Investigation: Carry out code linting and

investigation apparatuses to keep up with code quality.

Cooperative Apparatuses for Code Survey: Investigate devices like GitHub or GitLab for effective and cooperative code audits.

7. Best Practices for Python Security Common Security Vulnerabilities:

Identify and mitigate common Python code security flaws.

Secure Coding Practices: Follow best practices for composing secure Python code.

8. Getting Involved in Open Source Projects:

Contributing to Open Source Figure out how to add to open source projects and be essential for the Python people group.

Pull Demands and Code Commitment: Learn how to contribute code to open source repositories and submit pull requests.

9. Virtuoso Level Python People group

Drawing in with Python People group: Investigate on the web and disconnected networks where Python devotees and specialists assemble.

Meetings and Occasions: Network and stay up to date on the latest developments by attending Python conferences and events.

10. Suggested Books and Online journals

Books for Virtuoso Python Psyches: Investigate suggested books that cover progressed Python subjects.

Online resources and blogs: Follow compelling web journals and online assets for remaining informed and improving your Python abilities.

High level themes in Python give a pathway to ceaseless learning and dominance. By investigating these ideas, you'll extend how you might interpret the language as well as gain the abilities expected to handle mind boggling and complex tasks. How about we dig into the universe of cutting edge Python programming!

Best Practices for Virtuoso Level Python Advancement

As you raise your Python abilities to virtuoso level, embracing best practices becomes pivotal for composing viable, productive, and dependable code. This part covers a bunch of best practices that virtuoso level designers follow to create great Python code.

1. Code Construction and Association

Particular Plan: Figure out down your code into secluded parts with clear cut liabilities.

Bundle The board: Utilize virtual conditions and bundle directors like pip to oversee conditions.

Project Design: Understand a steady and intelligent venture structure for simple route.

2. Documentation Greatness

Docstrings: Compose exhaustive docstrings for modules, classes, and works to give in-code documentation.

README Documents: Create educational README documents with clear directions, project outline, and use models.

Utilization of Sphinx: Execute Sphinx to produce proficient and comprehensible documentation.

3. Adaptation Control and Joint effort

Git Best Practices: Follow Git best works on, including significant commit messages, stretching techniques, and regular commits.

Cooperative Instruments: Use cooperation devices like GitHub or GitLab for code survey, issue following, and undertaking the board.

4. Testing and Test-Driven Advancement (TDD)

Unit Testing: Compose careful unit tests for each capability and class to guarantee rightness.

Test Inclusion: In order to spot potential flaws and regressions, aim for high test coverage.

Persistent Joining (CI): Incorporate CI apparatuses like Travis CI or GitHub Activities for mechanized testing on each push.

5. Code Audit and Joint effort

Powerful Code Audits: Participate in and conduct efficient code reviews to identify issues early.

Criticism and Improvement: Give valuable input during code audits and be available to getting criticism.

Coding Principles: In order to keep the codebase consistent, enforce coding standards and style guides.

6. Execution Streamlining Strategies

Profiling Devices: Use profiling instruments to recognize and enhance execution bottlenecks.

Reserving Procedures: Carry out storing for as often as possible got to information to diminish calculation time.

Parallelism and Simultaneousness: Influence parallelism and simultaneousness for effective utilization of assets.

7. Security Mindfulness

Normal Security Practices: Follow security best works on, including input approval, secure coding, and keeping away from normal weaknesses.

Customary Security Reviews: Direct normal security reviews to distinguish and relieve likely dangers.

8. Continuous Education and Updating:

Learn about the most recent Python developments, libraries, and best practices.

Peruse and Add to Open Source: Learn from the community and contribute to open source projects.

9. Refactoring and optimizing code for readability:

Make code readability more important than cleverness.

Refactoring Practices: Routinely refactor code for practicality and further developed plan.

Reviews of code for optimization: Use code audits to distinguish and execute enhancement potential open doors.

10. Participate in Python Communities to Engage the Community:

Draw in with the Python people group through gatherings, gatherings, and meetups.

Share Information: Share your insight by composing blog entries, giving discussions, or adding to documentation.

By integrating these prescribed procedures into your work process, you'll compose code that functions as well as code that is effective, secure, and a delight to keep up with. Taking a stab at greatness in your improvement rehearses is critical to turning into a genuine virtuoso level Python engineer. Allow these prescribed procedures to direct you on your excursion to Python dominance!

Past Python: Reconciliations and Interoperability

As a virtuoso level Python engineer, extending your abilities to incorporate consistent mixes with different innovations and dialects is fundamental. This segment investigates methodologies and best practices for incorporating Python with different frameworks, data sets, and dialects, improving the interoperability of your tasks.

1. Communicating with Data sets

1.1 Social Information bases

SQLAlchemy ORM: Learn how to interact with relational databases using SQLAlchemy.

Data set Movements: Execute information base movements for overseeing outline changes over the long haul.

1.2 NoSQL Data sets

MongoDB and PyMongo: Utilize the PyMongo driver to investigate MongoDB integration.

Cassandra and DataStax Driver: Make use of the DataStax driver to learn how to work with the Cassandra NoSQL database.

2. Web APIs and Tranquil Administrations

2.1 Consuming APIs

Demands Library: Utilize the solicitations library to consume Soothing APIs.

Confirmation and OAuth: Carry out secure confirmation instruments while collaborating with APIs.

2.2 Structure APIs

Flagon Tranquil: Construct Soothing APIs utilizing Carafe and Cup Serene.

Django REST Structure: Use the Django REST Structure for making hearty APIs.

3. Message Line Frameworks

RabbitMQ and Celery: Utilize RabbitMQ and Celery to carry out asynchronous task processing.

Apache Kafka: Investigate reconciliation with Apache Kafka for dispersed occasion streaming.

4. JavaScript and AJAX integration with front-end technologies:

Incorporate Python applications with frontend innovations utilizing AJAX calls.

Frontend Structures: Work with famous frontend systems like Respond or Vue.js close by Python backend administrations.

5. Information Serialization Configurations

JSON and YAML: Ace serialization and deserialization of information in JSON and YAML designs.

Buffers and MessagePack for the Protocol: Investigate productive parallel serialization designs for information exchange.

6. Shell Scripting and Command-Line Interfaces (CLIs) Click and argparse:

Foster order line interfaces for Python applications utilizing Snap or argparse.

Shell Prearranging Mix: Join Python with shell scripts for mechanization and framework level undertakings.

7. Incorporating Python with C/C++ Code

Utilizing C Expansions: Incorporate Python with existing C code utilizing C expansions.

ctypes and Cython: Investigate options like ctypes and Cython for interacting with C libraries.

8. Cross-Language Interoperability

Python and Java Coordination: Investigate ways to combine Python code with Java code.

Utilizing C APIs from Python: Figure out how to interact with C APIs from Python applications.

9. Cloud Administration Reconciliations

AWS Boto3 and Sky blue SDK: Boto3 and the Azure SDK can be used to integrate with cloud services.

Serverless Registering: Carry out serverless capabilities utilizing stages like AWS Lambda or Google Cloud Capabilities.

10. Integration of Docker for Containerization and Orchestration:

Containerize Python applications involving Docker for conveyability.

Kubernetes Coordination: Investigate Kubernetes for arranging and scaling containerized applications.

11. AI Combination

TensorFlow and PyTorch: Incorporate Python with famous AI structures.

Scikit-Learn Pipelines: For seamless machine learning workflow integration, make use of Scikit-Learn pipelines.

12. Integration Error Handling and Logging Best Practices:

In integrated systems, implement robust error handling and logging mechanisms.

Observing and Examination: Use checking instruments and investigation to acquire experiences into incorporated frameworks' presentation.

By excelling at reconciliation and interoperability, you'll be exceptional to fabricate exhaustive arrangements that flawlessly associate with different advances and administrations. These abilities are fundamental for making flexible and adaptable applications that can flourish in different conditions. Allow these systems to direct you in broadening the range of your Python projects past the limits of the language.

Genuine Applications and Contextual analyses

Gaining from genuine applications and contextual analyses is a phenomenal method for understanding how to apply your Python abilities in functional situations. This section looks at real-world use cases and case studies that show how Python is used in different fields and industries.

1. Information Investigation and Representation

1.1 Monetary Information Investigation

Stock Value Forecast: Utilize authentic stock value information to anticipate future stock costs utilizing AI models.

Portfolio Improvement: Execute calculations to upgrade venture portfolios in light of chance and return.

1.2 Showcasing Examination

Client Division: Identify segments for targeted marketing campaigns by analyzing customer data.

Beat Expectation: Anticipate client stir and carry out techniques to hold important clients.

2. Medical care and Life Sciences

2.1 Clinical Picture Examination

X-ray Picture Division: Foster calculations for dividing and examining structures in clinical X-ray pictures.

Sickness Recognition: Use AI for early identification of illnesses in light of clinical information.

2.2 Medication Disclosure

Chemoinformatics: Apply computational techniques to examine synthetic information for drug disclosure.

AI in Pharmacology: Use AI models to anticipate drug associations and incidental effects.

3. Internet business and Retail

3.1 Recommender Frameworks

Item Proposals: Assemble recommender frameworks for proposing items to clients in light of their inclinations.

Customized Shopping Experience: Carry out calculations to customize the shopping experience for clients.

3.2 Store network Improvement

Request Estimating: Utilize verifiable information for anticipating item interest and upgrading stock.

Course Advancement: Carry out calculations for streamlining conveyance courses and diminishing transportation costs.

4. Web Advancement and Applications

4.1 Substance The board Frameworks

Building a Writing for a blog Stage: Create a blogging-friendly content management system with publishing and creation capabilities.

Internet business Stages: Assemble adaptable web based business stages with highlights like item postings, shopping baskets, and request handling.

4.2 Online Entertainment Investigation

Feeling Investigation: Examine online entertainment information to grasp feeling around items or brands.

Analyses of User Behavior: Use examination to grasp client conduct and inclinations via virtual entertainment stages.

5. 5.1 Smart Home Systems Home Automation:

Internet of Things (IoT) Make a shrewd home framework that permits clients to remotely control gadgets.

Energy Utilization Observing: Execute IoT answers for observing and improving energy utilization in homes.

5.2 Modern IoT

Prescient Upkeep: Use IoT sensors and AI to anticipate gear disappointments in modern settings.

Remote Observing and Control: Execute frameworks for remotely checking and controlling modern cycles.

6. Instruction and E-Learning

6.1 Learning The board Frameworks

Online Course Stages: Foster stages for facilitating and overseeing on the web courses.

Versatile Learning Frameworks: Execute versatile learning frameworks that customize instructive substance in light of understudy progress.

6.2 Normal Language Handling in Training

Computerized Reviewing Frameworks: Utilize normal language handling for mechanizing the evaluating of composed tasks.

Clever Coaching Frameworks: Assemble frameworks that give customized mentoring in light of understudy execution.

The adaptability and power of Python across a variety of industries are demonstrated in these real-world applications and case studies. As you investigate these models, you'll acquire bits of knowledge into how Python is applied to tackle complex issues and make inventive arrangements. Think about these cases as motivation for your own undertakings and attempts in the thrilling universe of Python advancement.

Congratulations on reaching the guide's

Conclusion,

"Python for Genius Minds!" All through this far reaching venture, you've dove into the profundities of Python programming, from the essentials to cutting edge subjects, and investigated its applications across different spaces. As you think about your learning, here are key important points:

1. A Strong Groundwork

You've laid out areas of strength for an in Python programming, dominating fundamental ideas, for example, factors, information types, control stream, capabilities, from there, the sky is the limit. This establishment fills in as the structure blocks for your high level investigation.

2. High level Python Ideas

You've extended your Python ability into cutting edge regions, including object-situated programming, practical programming, simultaneousness, and metaprogramming. These high level subjects engage you to compose more effective, rich, and adaptable code.

3. Information Science and AI

You've wandered into the domain of information science and AI, gaining abilities in information control, perception, and model turn of events. This information positions you to handle genuine issues and concentrate significant bits of knowledge from information.

4. Web Improvement with Carafe and Django

You've investigated web improvement utilizing two famous systems, Cup and Django, acquiring the capacity to construct dynamic and component rich web applications. From making Soothing APIs to incorporating with data sets, you've taken in the intricate details of web advancement.

5. Past Python: Combinations and Interoperability

You've extended your points of view by investigating how Python incorporates with different innovations, information bases, dialects, and administrations. This information prepares you to make exhaustive arrangements that flawlessly associate with different frameworks.

6. Best Practices and Certifiable Applications

You've embraced prescribed procedures for virtuoso level turn of events, including code structure, documentation, testing, and cooperation. Genuine applications and contextual analyses have given you bits of knowledge into applying your Python abilities across different enterprises.

7. Continuous Education

Keeping up with the latest developments in technology necessitates ongoing education. To stay sharp and creative, participate in the Python community, contribute to open source projects, and investigate new technologies.

Keep in mind that programming is more than just writing code as you progress through the Python course; it's tied in with taking care of issues, making rich arrangements, and adding to the more extensive local area. Whether you're building web applications, breaking down information, or diving into AI, Python enables you to rejuvenate your thoughts.

Continue coding, investigating, and pushing the limits of what you can accomplish with Python. This is not the end of the journey; it develops with each line of code you compose and each issue you settle. May your Python undertakings keep on being loaded up with imagination, advancement, and the delight of building striking arrangements.